Around
Mildenhall

IN OLD PHOTOGRAPHS

The market cross, 1905. The cross has dominated the market-place since the fifteenth century. It is still nominally owned by the lord of the manor of Mildenhall, but since 1938 has been leased to the parish council at a peppercorn rent. The shop on the left was then the Cash Boot Stores. Harry Ungless had the shop on the right from 1898 until his death in 1906; previously it had been the Pettit bakery. (Mildenhall Museum)

Around
Mildenhall

IN OLD PHOTOGRAPHS

COLIN M. DRING

Alan Sutton Publishing Limited
Phoenix Mill · Far Thrupp · Stroud
Gloucestershire

First Published 1994

British Library Cataloguing in Publication Data.
A catalogue record for this book is available from
the British Library.

ISBN 0-7509-0796-7

Typeset in 9/10 Sabon.
Typesetting and origination by
Alan Sutton Publishing Limited.
Printed in Great Britain by
The Guernsey Press Company Limited,
Guernsey, Channel Islands.

Contents

The Clarke brothers stacking barley at The Elms, West Row, *c.* 1910. Arthur is standing on the cart with Adolphus Herbert on the left and Charles on the right. Until recent times almost the entire population of the area was employed in farming and related trades. (Mildenhall Museum)

Introduction

The history of the small market town of Mildenhall can be traced back to Anglo-Saxon times although nothing remains of the original settlement except for a large cemetery just outside the limits of the present town. The Domesday survey of 1086 recorded that the town was well established with a church, a mill and a total of sixty-four families, not to mention a flock of a thousand sheep. The whole of the manor of Mildenhall belonged to the abbey of Bury St Edmunds and the abbot had total control over the area, including the right to hang criminals in the market-place. On a less macabre note, a weekly market on Fridays has been held regularly since 1412 when a royal charter for this was first granted. An annual two-day timber and servant hiring fair was also held on Fair Spot Field, the site of the present Riverside School, until about 1850.

The manor of Mildenhall was confiscated by the Crown at the dissolution of the monasteries in 1536 and later sold to Sir Roger North of Kirtling, whose son Henry settled in Mildenhall soon after 1586 and built the manor house. The estate passed through four generations of the North family, some of whom were prominent in national politics and all of whom were staunch royalists – King Charles II stayed at the manor during one of his regular visits to Newmarket. The last of the local Norths, Sir Henry, was a melancholy man who shot himself in the manor house in 1671 but, being lord of the manor, was buried in the parish church rather than in unconsecrated ground as was normal then for suicides. The estate passed to Sir Thomas Hanmer, Henry's nephew, who became a famous speaker of the House of Commons. Sir Thomas extended the manor house and gave the town four almshouses and a workhouse, all in the churchyard. It is said that he married twice, once for love and once for money but was successful in neither: his second wife eloped with his cousin, Thomas Hervey. Sir William Bunbury, Hanmer's nephew, inherited in 1747 and Mildenhall remained in the hands of this family until the final break up of the estate in 1933. Legend has it that in 1780 Sir Thomas Charles Bunbury tossed a coin with Lord Derby to decide whose name should be given to a new race. Derby won the toss but Bunbury's horse won the first Derby.

The ancient parish of Mildenhall, which included the hamlets of Beck Row, Holywell Row, Kenny Hill and West Row, covered 17,000 acres and was the largest in Suffolk. The parish was so extensive because much of the land was of marginal value and a large area was required to support the population. The following account by the 2nd Earl of Oxford, who was clearly not impressed by the area, gives a graphic description of the landscape in the eighteenth century:

> The next day Thursday, September the 21st, 1732, we set out from Brandon, seven long, very long miles to Barton Mills over the sands, terrible tedious travelling both to man and horse. I could not but reflect what terrible travelling it must be where the heat of the sun is intense upon the wide sandy deserts, where the poor travellers are often smothered with the sand or scorched with the sun's heat reflected from the burning sands. We leave the sands at Barton Mills which we were very glad of. The river that runs by Barton Mills is navigable as I said to Bury. We left Mildenhall, the seat of Sir Thomas Hanmer, on the right hand, a most miserable situation. On one side he is subject to be choked with sand, on the other he lives close to a dark vile black fen which lies to the north east of him; so that he enjoys that wicked wind with the addition of the air from that fen.

The landscape has changed much since then. The fens have been drained and now comprise some of the most fertile land in the country. The dry Breckland area, formerly used mainly as rabbit warrens and sheep walks before becoming vast sporting estates, is now largely covered by the plantations of the Forestry Commission. Ancient man evidently found the region much more congenial than did the Earl of Oxford for there has been life here for at least half a million years, the date confidently ascribed to the traces of Old Stone Age man found at High Lodge, just outside Mildenhall. The combination of the marshy fenland and the dry, easily tilled, Breckland was favourable to hunting and early farming so it is not surprising that so many traces of settlement, from the Old Stone Age onwards, have been found in the vicinity. The Romans had a ring of farmsteads around the fen edge and the fabulous Mildenhall Treasure, thirty-two pieces of silver tableware now in the British Museum, was discovered near one of these during the Second World War. Another Roman hoard, this time of pewter, was discovered in 1962 when the remains of a crashed wartime bomber were being excavated.

The economy of the town and the surrounding villages has, until recent times, been based almost solely on agriculture and Mildenhall has figured little in national history. However, in 1144 Geoffrey de Mandeville, the archetypal robber baron who changed sides frequently during the troubled reign of King Stephen, made the mistake of taking off his helmet to cool down while besieging the unfinished castle at nearby Burwell. He was struck by an arrow and retired wounded to die at Mildenhall. Then, during the 1381 Peasants' Uprising, John de Cambridge, the prior of the abbey at Bury St Edmunds, was murdered on Mildenhall Heath. Apart from such events as these the town lay low for centuries. The old open fields were enclosed in 1812 but the area suffered greatly during the agricultural depression of the later nineteenth century. The main London to Norwich railway could have come through Mildenhall but this was opposed by the local gentry; it was not until 1885 that a branch line from Cambridge appeared, but this was too late and too little to allow the town to expand to any extent, and finally closed in 1964.

All began to change in 1931 when Mildenhall was selected to be the home of the first of the Royal Air Force's new style bomber bases. Building began then and the base was officially opened in 1934, just after the famous Great Air Race from Mildenhall to Melbourne, Australia had started from here on 20 October 1934. The race attracted enormous international interest and Mildenhall was at last in the limelight. Crowds came to see such famous fliers as Amy Johnson and there were traffic jams for miles around on the actual starting day. The race was won by a de Havilland Comet, flown by C.W.A. Scott and T. Campbell Black, who reached Australia in less than seventy-two hours, an incredible feat for those days. The airfield was also in the news in 1935 when King George V, accompanied by his sons the Prince of Wales and the Duke of York, came for the first ever full review of the Royal Air Force in honour of the king's silver jubilee. RAF Mildenhall was an important British bomber base during the Second World War but, since 1950, has been home to the United States Air Force and is now one of the most important American installations in this country. Crowds in their hundreds of thousands attend the annual two-day air fêtes which are now an established feature of life in the area.

The arrival of the air force started to improve the economy but major development did not come until the 1960s when an agreement was reached with the Greater London Council to move families here from London. Many new houses were built and a light industrial estate established to provide employment for the newcomers. The town now has a secure industrial base and can face the future with some confidence.

The choice of subject matter in this book has been dictated by the availability of photographs. More and more are coming to light as interest in the past increases but, unfortunately, many roads and institutions are not represented as no material has yet emerged. One hopes this will be rectified in future works. No attempt has been made to include RAF Mildenhall or the Cambridge to Mildenhall railway as these are already covered by books that remain in print.

SECTION ONE
Mildenhall

The first section of the book deals with the town of Mildenhall which, strictly speaking, should be called the High Town to distinguish it from the ancient parish of Mildenhall which used to include the Rows. Never, please, refer to it as Mildenhall village. Several of the photographs depict shops festooned with flowers as part of the annual July flower show celebrations. These shows were held every year from 1873 to 1912 and again from 1924 until the 1940s. Special trains were laid on to bring visitors from Cambridge and a committee, for long run by Mr Fortescue of The White Hart, met throughout the year to raise money to pay for the decorations which became ever more elaborate year by year. Mildenhall Lions now organize an annual carnival to raise money for charity but the exuberance of the old days is, sadly, lacking.

Police Station Square, c. 1908. The war memorial was erected on the green in 1920. Shrublands House can be seen on the left and the wall of Pound Close on the right. The police station and courthouse were built in 1851 but the police have been based at the new station in Kingsway since 1970. (Mildenhall Museum)

The Market Square, 1890s. First on the right is Jonathan Norman's butcher's shop, now the Market Cross Surgery. Isaac Minns' saddlery shop is hidden by the water pump. Then come Stiles the outfitters, the Pettit bakery and, on the corner, the Cash Boot Stores. (Mildenhall Museum)

Another view of the Market Square, 1890s. The building in the right-hand corner, for long a stationer's, was rebuilt in 1905 and is now the Eastern Electricity showroom. The building on the left has since been extended at both ends. (Spanton-Jarman collection)

Mr R. Clarke the builder's house at the top of the Market Square, decorated for the annual flower show in 1906. This is now the Nationwide Building Society. The façade is original but the main part of the house was rebuilt in the early 1970s. (Mr W. Bell)

One of the carts belonging to Mr Clarke, seen here in Station Road. William Croft is driving and George 'Yankee' Ashman is on the side. The beautiful black horses were much in demand for funerals and also pulled the town fire engine. (Mildenhall Museum)

The High Street, *c.* 1908. Barclays Bank, now the TSB, is on the corner. Next comes the old White Hart and then an ironmonger's shop, at this time run by Mr E.J. Mutton who also had a smithy in St Andrew's Street. (Mildenhall Museum)

Outside the bank, 1890s. Gurney's and Co. traded here from the early 1870s but, as a result of mergers and family connections, became Barclays in 1907. The little shop on the right was then the off-licence for the White Hart; later it became Mrs Judkin's sweet shop, but it is now again part of the hotel. (Mr L. Reeve)

The old White Hart, 1895. William Willson was the proprietor from 1889, taking over from Mr J. Fortescue who had been landlord for over twenty years. The old pub had three storeys but was rebuilt with only two. (Mr L. Reeve)

The fire at the White Hart, 28 April 1910. The hotel, one of the oldest buildings in the town, was totally destroyed. Some features of the old hostelry, in particular the hay racks on the wall, can still be seen in the yard at the back. (Mildenhall Museum)

The Bell Hotel, decorated for an early flower show. Note the archway giving access to the yard; this has since been closed in to make the main entrance to the hotel. The front of the White Hart shows that this must be later than 1910. (Mildenhall Museum)

The High Street, 1950s. Bussens and Parkin reopened the ironmongery shop, which had been empty for some years, in 1928 but in 1968, following a disastrous fire, moved to their present premises in King Street. (Mr W. Bell)

The town was decorated for the coronation of King George V on 22 June 1911 but the High Street looks strangely deserted for such an important day. Many flags are on display but the exuberance of the flower show decorations is missing. (Mr L. Reeve)

The coronation tea in the Town Hall on 22 June 1911, the reason why the High Street was so empty. The Town Hall in St Andrew's Street was built in 1886 and, until its demolition in 1987, was the base for most of the town's celebrations and amateur dramatics. (Mr L. Reeve)

The High Street, 1890s. First on the left is Morley's, then a watchmaker and jeweller. Then come two shops run by the Stiles family; these were incorporated into Morley's in 1933. On the corner is Mr Williams' grocery shop. All these were part of the old Cock Inn until 1821. (Spanton-Jarman collection)

Another view of the High Street, 1890s. First on the right is a butcher's shop, run then by Harry Randall, but the same trade had been carried on here at least since 1711, when John Shafton and two of his children died in a smallpox epidemic. (Spanton-Jarman collection)

The High Street, 1927. Westgate & Sons, seed merchants, occupied the whole of the corner block, but in 1928 Mr R.A. Lack opened his tobacconist's shop on the corner of St Andrew's Street. Earlier this had been the Junction House bakery. (Mr W. Bell)

An early view of St Andrew's Street showing the Town Hall on the right. This street was called Cock Inn Lane until that inn closed in 1821. In 1895 it was found that the parish church was originally dedicated to St Mary. The name of the church was changed but not that of the street. (Mr L. Reeve)

Mill Street, 1896. On the left, surrounded by railings, is Clinton House, then a doctor's house and surgery. On the right the high wall surrounds the grounds of the house known as the Arboretum, now the Riverside Hotel. (Spanton-Jarman collection)

Further down Mill Street on the same day. The first house on the left was once a pub, known in the eighteenth century as the Black Horse and later as the King's Head. By 1896 it was the home of Frank Parker, an auctioneer. (Spanton-Jarman collection)

The top of Mill Street, 1896. On the left is the Simpson stationery shop and printing works. This block of small shops and cottages was demolished in the 1960s but all the other shops and houses remain. (Spanton-Jarman collection)

Mill Street on 6 July 1935 as King George V, accompanied by his two sons who were both to become kings, visited RAF Mildenhall for the first ever full review of the Royal Air Force, to mark the occasion of his silver jubilee. (Mildenhall Museum)

An early view of the south side of Mill Street showing Pettit's steam bakery in what is now Starling's Nest. This was once the post office – note the post box. The house on the right, now Swift Print, was then occupied by the housekeeper for the adjacent property, which was known as The Homestead. (Mr L. Reeve)

The Model T Ford delivery van belonging to the Pettit bakery. On the left is Charlie Youngs and on the right Ezra Human. All the local shops were only too keen to deliver to regular customers. (Mr R. Youngs)

The south side of Mill Street, 1920s. The building on the right was run by the Misses Hills as the town's first telephone exchange. Next was Ecclestone's drapery store, the shop window of which has since been extended to the pavement. (Mr L. Reeve)

The International Stores opened in Mill Street in 1909 and remained there until 1976. Potter's wine and spirits shop was sold to Mothersoles in 1910 and later merged into the International's premises. (Mr L. Reeve)

A traction engine belonging to Favor Parker leaving Mill Street, 1908. This photograph was taken on the engine's first working day as it went to Peterhouse Farm at Undley. It was a Burrell 7 hp single crank compound engine and one of three sets owned by Favor Parker. The driver is Ted Fincham and the boy by the wheel is probably Spencer Parker. The man in the straw boater is probably Herbert Rudland, standing by the gate of his newly opened coal yard. Note the plain sash windows of the house on the left, 20 Mill Street; they are now bow windows. The same buildings are portrayed a little later in the photographs opposite. (Mr A.J. Thompson)

A decorated cart outside 18 Mill Street, then the premises of Mr L.W. Wallis, the local photographer who took many of the photographs that appear in this book. Standing are Bessie Fincham and David Butcher. (Mr W. Bell)

The same premises, December 1928. Mr Webb from Exning had opened a garage here in 1925. Note how the wall is cut back diagonally to accommodate the petrol pump; this feature can still be seen today. (Mildenhall Museum)

An early view of the Tiger's Head in the High Street. (Mr F. Locke)

The yard of the Bell Hotel soon after Mr and Mrs Harry Smith took over from Mr and Mrs William Booty in 1921. (Mr F. Locke)

Miss Ivy Goodrem at work in 1934. Ivy took over the family coal merchant's business when her father died and ran it almost single-handed for some ten years until she married. She has since, as Mrs Base, been well known in the area, particularly for her long association with the Bunbury Players. The coal yard was at the beginning of Kingsway, backing on to the premises now occupied by Bussens and Parkin. Mildenhall was in the limelight in 1934 as the England to Australia Great Air Race started from the newly opened aerodrome. Crowds came to see Amy Johnson and other famous fliers prepare for the race. On the actual starting day, 20 October, there was a traffic jam for miles around. Ivy was spotted by Pathé News and appeared on cinema newsreels. As a result of this she was invited to appear on the BBC programme *In Town Tonight*. (Mildenhall Museum)

The almshouses in the churchyard, 1909. These were given to the town by Sir Thomas Hanmer, Speaker of the House of Commons and Lord of Mildenhall Manor, in 1722. They were restored by Mildenhall Round Table in 1978. (Mr F. Locke)

Mrs Annie Norman outside her cottage in the churchyard, c. 1930. These three-storey cottages were knocked down to make way for the present employment exchange in the 1960s. (Mr W. Bell)

A lithograph of the parish church by James Scales, 1825. The east window soars high above the then flat chancel roof; the window was restored and the roof raised to its original height in 1851. The small lantern spire was removed in about 1830. (Mildenhall Museum)

The interior of the church in about 1840 showing the old box pews and reading desk in front of the Jacobean pulpit, part of which is now in Beck Row church. New pews were installed during the 1851 restoration but the present pews date from 1959. (Mildenhall Museum)

The vicarage in Queensway, 1913. The old vicarage in the market-place, where Leo's supermarket now stands, was given to the Church by the lord of the manor in 1746 and sold in 1876 when the new vicarage was built. (Mildenhall Museum)

A Mothers' Union group in the garden of the Queensway vicarage, 26 June 1914. The minister in the middle of the back row must be the Revd William Henry Wood. This building has since been converted into flats. (Mr L. Reeve)

Mildenhall's Elizabethan manor house, *c.* 1898. This was built by Sir Henry North in about 1586 and extended by Sir Thomas Hanmer in the eighteenth century. One room was called the King Charles room to commemorate a visit from Charles II. The house was leased from 1897 until 1903, while the Bunburys were living at their Great Barton estate, to the Society of the Sacred Mission as a training college for missionaries. Sir Henry Bunbury's girls' school continued to meet in the great hall throughout this time. The property was included in the final 1933 auction of the Bunbury estates and, sadly, demolished. Some of the Tudor wall paintings were bought by the Victoria and Albert Museum. Many of the houses on the south side of Queensway were occupied by members of the manor house staff. Nothing remains of the Elizabethan structure, but an interesting earlier, probably fourteenth-century, building still stands on private land off Church Lane. This was a *columbarium* for the intensive rearing of pigeons for food. (Mildenhall Museum)

West Street, before the First World War. The wall and gates of the manor house can be seen on the left. The street was renamed Queensway to commemorate the coronation of Queen Elizabeth II in 1953. (Mildenhall Museum)

Westway Cottages in Queensway, *c.* 1900. An upper storey was added in the 1930s. A silk manufactory, run by Grant, Baylis and Co. of Norwich, flourished here in the 1830s but the building later came to be used as a lodging house. (Mr R. Youngs)

Wamil Way, *c.* 1917. On the left is Lily Brown, later Mrs Harry Halls; on the right is May Rolfe who married Frank Ford, the West Row engineer. The lady in the doorway is Mrs Dick Dodd. The town bridewell, or small prison, was in this street. (Mr W. Bell)

Bill Morley holding the pony of a decorated cart in Queensway, *c.* 1908. On the left is the yard of the Queen's Arms and on the right is The Yews. Queens Drive was cut through here in the 1960s. (Mr W. Bell)

Police Station Square, with the war memorial and the gardens of The Thatched House in the background, 1930s. Pound Meadow, not then developed, is on the left. (Mr F. Locke)

Police Station Square, looking up North Terrace, probably in 1926 when Simpson was complaining of the green being used as a dumping ground. In the centre, at the end of the wall, is the fire engine house just before Toombs' garage. (Mr W. Bell)

North Terrace, *c.* 1930. The Comet cinema, named after the winner of the Great Air Race, was built on part of the Pound Close in 1935 and the new fire station was built alongside in the early 1950s. (Mr W. Bell)

North Terrace, when the large house on the left, nowadays hidden by hedges, was the home and surgery of Dr Howard Glazier, July 1908. The Jehovah Jireh strict Calvinist chapel once stood in the gardens of the house. (Mr L. Reeve)

The town fire brigade, 1937. Standing, left to right: Constable Smith, C. Pledger, R. Carter, O. Snushall, T. Locke, J. Carter, S. Bonnett, R. Beckett, G. Kidd, Sergeant Last. Sitting: C. Gee, Dr Capel, Commander Ord, H.E. Turner, William Clarke. The volunteer fire brigade was formed in 1889 and the engine was kept in a shed between the courthouse and the garage in North Terrace. The first firemen to arrive had to collect the keys from the police station in the courthouse and then send a man off to collect Mr Clarke's horses to pull the engine. A steam engine was bought in 1921 but it was not until 1936 that the brigade had its first motorized unit, as seen here, a gift from the Greene King brewery in Bury St Edmunds. (Mildenhall Museum)

The fire brigade, 1890s. The man on the horse is Samuel Garnham Reeve, superintendent of police for the Lackford Division based at Mildenhall. This engine performed badly at the 1921 Bridge Mill fire (see p. 43) and was replaced by a steam engine. (Spanton-Jarman collection)

This photograph of 30 April 1944 suggests that the wartime fire brigade had won a competition. At the back on the left is Fred Locke and on the right Reg Wallis. Sitting, from the left, are Bill Butcher, George Kidd and Dick Morley. (Mr F. Locke)

Samuel Turner outside his butcher's shop on the corner of Market Street and King Street. Mr Turner had managed the shop for the Boyces but took over in his own right in 1915. (Mr W. Bell)

The cottages on the corner of King Street and Market Street in 1982, just before their renovation and conversion to become Mildenhall Museum. The two entrances in Market Street have been blocked in and a large extension, covering the site of two wells, built at the rear. (Mildenhall Museum)

A carriage, probably for a wedding, outside The Thatched House, at the corner of King Street and Kingsway, in 1967. This, the last thatched building in Mildenhall, was knocked down in 1970 to make way for new houses. (Mildenhall Museum)

The Maid's Head in Kingsway, decorated for the annual flower show, c. 1900. Outside are Mr and Mrs F. Vale, the licensees, with their family and staff. (Mildenhall Museum)

Kingsway, early 1900s. This road was originally called the Neatway, later Kiln Street and then Cemetery Road, but only the postcard salesman ever called it the Newmarket Road. (Mr W. Bell)

Further along Kingsway, *c.* 1908. The cottages on the left have been restored in recent years. The trees were planted for Edward VII's coronation in 1902, but little development occurred until building plots were made available in 1932. (Mildenhall Museum)

The Mildenhall Union Workhouse, as demolition started in 1924. This was built for £11,000 in 1895, replacing the workhouse in the churchyard. It was taken over by the army during the First World War and never used as a workhouse again, being finally sold for only £2,250 in 1924. The police station now occupies part of this site. (Mildenhall Museum)

Half Moon Corner, early 1900s. The Brandon road was obviously far more important than the Bury road at this time. (Mildenhall Museum)

The Thetford Road wood yard, *c*. 1922. The driver of the Burrell general purpose engine is Arthur Gage and Freeman Gage is the steersman. William Ford is standing in the centre. This wood yard closed in 1922. (Mr A.J. Thompson)

This view, probably from the early 1920s, shows the old cottages standing back from the Bury Road on the land now occupied by Hazel Close. (Mr W. Bell)

A group of farmworkers on Wamil Farm, 1893. Back row, left to right: R. Lock, Cole, H. Thompson, Nunn, A. Thompson, Watkinson. Middle: Watkinson, -?-, Abrey, J. Abrey, C. Brown, Kidd (the one-armed gamekeeper). Front: Turner, yet another Watkinson, Brown, Abbott. The majority of folk, in Mildenhall as well as in the villages, were employed in agriculture until the advent of mechanization. (Mr A.J. Thompson)

The Ship in Mill Street, 1950s. This closed in 1983 and the whole structure was dismantled and rebuilt further back from the road. It was found to be based on a medieval hall and is probably the oldest surviving building in the town. (Mr F. Locke)

A view of the river from the town quay before the First World War. The river was allowed to silt up after the coming of the railway in 1885 but the Eastern Counties Navigation and Transport Co. opened up the navigation again for a short period in the 1890s. (Mildenhall Museum)

This view from the bridge was used as a Christmas card in 1906. Part of the Bridge Mill can be seen on the left and two locks are visible downstream. The Mallards, a private development of sheltered houses for the elderly, was built in the fields on the right in the 1980s. (Mr R. Youngs)

Bridge Mill, then owned by Parker Brothers, burned down on 21 August 1921. The town's horse-drawn hand-operated pump, seen on the left, failed to cope with the fire and was soon replaced by a steam engine, still horse-drawn. (Mildenhall Museum)

This very early photograph shows a horse pulling a pair of barges along the Lark. This was the usual means of propulsion at the time. Barges used to bring goods from King's Lynn to Mildenhall and onwards to Bury St Edmunds. (Mildenhall Museum)

The Lark Angling & Preservation Society restocking the river with fish at the Gas Pool, c. 1930. The man on the far right is Major Neve. The town gasworks was opened in 1840 but was closed in 1958 and demolished in the 1970s. (Mildenhall Museum)

A gala and aquatic fête was held in 1889 and this shows one of the decorated boats by the bank of the Lark at the back of what was then Cocksedge's yard, now St Mary's Close. The Williams family is in the boat and the small boy in the middle is Maurice Williams, who later took over his father's grocery shop in the High Street. He was scoutmaster from 1921 to 1970, emerging from a well-earned retirement to lay the foundation stone for the new scout hut in 1980. (Mildenhall Museum)

King's Staunch, on the Lark near Wamil Hall, soon after this flash lock had been rebuilt in the 1890s. The river is now navigable only as far as Judes Ferry. (Mildenhall Museum)

Wamil Hall before the fire of 1912. Once an independent manor, Wamil was amalgamated with the main Mildenhall estate in 1754. In the 1890s Rosamond Lyell, a niece of Lady Bunbury, had use of the hall as a home for children from London. (Mildenhall Museum)

The fire at Wamil Hall, 29 November 1912. Major rebuilding was necessary but the bulk of the old house, built by Sir Henry Warner in the 1500s, was saved.

A sports day at Wamil Hall, early 1900s. Many local groups, including the West Row church Sunday school, were allowed to make use of these delightful grounds for their annual celebrations. (Mildenhall Museum)

The Mildenhall mixed hockey team, taken on Pound Meadow where the fire station now stands, 21 February 1914. Back row, left to right: T.V.P. Shields, M. Turner, B. Falkenstein, Maurice Williams, M. Simpson, W.G. Stockley (referee), D.M.P. Shields, J.S. Watson. Middle: M. Ward (vice-captain), C. Stebbing (captain), M. Stockley. Miss E. Pettit, from the High Street bakery, is sitting at the front. Mr Stockley was the headmaster of Mildenhall Infants' School. (Mildenhall Museum)

The Football Club in festive spirit, Christmas Day 1920. The town's first club was formed in September 1879 and the game, after some early setbacks, has been flourishing here ever since. Standing, left to right: Bill Jakes, Fred Simpson, Bill Hutchinson, Joe Hunt, Seymour Youngs, Charlie Ranns, Archie Morley, Sid Palmer, -?-, Tom Adams, Jack Tabner. Seated: -?-, Gordon Parker, Sid Frost, O.H. Read, 'Fluff' Stiles, Billy Hood, Arthur Bond, Bert Wells, -?-, -?-. (Mr R. Youngs)

This delightful Victorian photograph came from the collections of the Stiles family, local shopkeepers until 1933. It probably shows Mildenhall's first cycling club, started in 1894 with Dr William Dunn, a local GP, as president. (Mildenhall Museum)

Group four of the Mildenhall Boys' School, June 1894. The headmaster, Mr W.G. Stockley, is seated on the left with his daughter Etheldreda on his lap. He was headmaster from 1893, taking over from his father-in-law, John L. Saxton, who had held the post for forty years. At this time the Boys' School was held in the Bunbury Rooms and the girls met in the great hall of the manor house. In 1902 both schools, still as separate boys' and girls' departments, moved to North Terrace when St Mary's C. of E. Aided Primary School was built. Mr Stockley continued as headmaster of both wings of the school until 1921. (Mildenhall Museum)

The Mildenhall branch of the Church Lads' Brigade, 1908. This detachment started in 1899 and is still, as the Boys' Brigade, a flourishing youth organization. It meets at the Baptist chapel but is open to boys from all denominations. (Mr L. Reeve)

The mobilization of the Territorial Army on 5 August 1914 with Stanley Parker leading the march. All important events were marked by processions through the town, usually with the fire brigade at the head of the parade. (Mr L. Reeve)

The Radio Frolics concert party was started in 1936 and lasted until the Second World War. Back row, left to right: Trevor Hagger, Lionel Byron, Ken Forman, Sid Stebbeds. Middle: Peggy Lark, Vera Woollard, Stella Bryant. Cecil Butcher is sitting at the front. This group was much in demand throughout the area but ceased activity with the outbreak of war. In the post-war period the Toc H performed annual pantomimes, giving way to the Mildenhall Singers and Players and then to the Bunbury Players, who still continue the long tradition of amateur dramatics in the town. (Mildenhall Museum)

SECTION TWO
Barton Mills

Barton Mills, also known in early times as Barton Parva, is a large and thriving village just 1 mile from Mildenhall. Alexander Fleming, the discoverer of penicillin, lived here during the Second World War. The main A11 London road skirts the village and, fortunately, there have been far fewer serious accidents since the major improvements of the 1980s. Road fatalities are nothing new, for Simpson writes of Chalk Hill, 'where the road is cut between high chalk cliffs, memorable from the frightful mail-coach accident of years bygone, which precipitated the whole of the passengers into a deep and awful gulf, from which it is said not a soul escaped with life, the four horses sharing the same fate'.

A peaceful scene at Fiveways crossroads in the 1920s, long before the roundabout was built in the early 1950s. The AA man on duty is probably 'Chiefie' Smith. (Mildenhall Museum)

The mill, 1920s. The lane here used to be the main London to Norwich road but is now a quiet cul-de-sac. The mill was demolished in 1948 after having been derelict for some years. (Mildenhall Museum)

Another view of the mill, 1890s. Abraham Peachey was the miller in the 1860s but by the 1890s the business was in the hands of Mr J.H. Godfery, whose son Walter took over in 1909. (Mildenhall Museum)

The courtyard of the Bull soon after Mr G.S. Peeling replaced Mr H.W. Moore as landlord in 1908. Mr Peeling worked hard to restore this old coaching inn to some of its former glory. (Mildenhall Museum)

The A11, 1930s. Mill House remains on the left as does Larkspur Cottage on the right. The mill itself can be seen behind Larkspur Cottage. The iron railings around Mill House were removed for scrap during the Second World War. (Mildenhall Museum)

Ernest Webb's garage, 1930s. Mr Webb from Exning opened a garage here on the old London road in 1924 and the following year opened a garage in Mildenhall. AJ's restaurant now occupies this site. (Mr W. Bell)

Chaff cutting at Street Farm when John Carpenter had the farm, 1 March 1910. Mr Sandford's house can be seen in the background. Modern houses now stand in the farmyard. (Mildenhall Museum)

An accident in the early 1930s. This Foden steam lorry from Norwich had stopped to draw up water from the river by the little bridge outside Webb's garage on the old main road. Its wheels went through the bridge and it could not be moved. W.J. Ford and Sons, the agricultural engineers in West Row, had to send a traction engine to pull it out. Sergeant Hurrell from Mildenhall police station is busy taking notes. (Mildenhall Museum)

The Butcher family at Bridgeman's Row, *c.* 1915. Standing, left to right: Nellie Butcher (later Mrs Cadman), Elias Drake, Nancy Hannah Butcher (Mrs Lynn), Polly Mary Ann Butcher (Mrs Drake), Mr William Butcher, a painter and decorator. Sitting: Mrs Eunice Drake, Bessie Drake (Mrs George Locke), Mrs Mary Butcher, née Drake. This row of cottages was demolished in about 1978. (Mrs M.O. Jennings)

The Dog and Partridge, early 1900s. Mrs Alice Westley was killed when the pub was almost totally destroyed by a fire on 25 January 1959. A thatched roof was then discovered under the tiles. (Mildenhall Museum)

Grange Lane, also known as Workers' Lane, before the First World War. The cottages on the left were pulled down in 1956 and that on the right burned down in about 1930, but the house in the far distance still stands in Church Lane. (Mildenhall Museum)

Constable Futter from Mildenhall controlling traffic outside the Sandfords' nursery, 1950s. Crowds came from far and wide to see the dahlia gardens when they were opened for charity each year. (Mildenhall Museum)

The Turners' bakehouse, with Charles and Susie Turner in the garden and Doris (later Mrs Sowerby) by the car, c. 1930. Business ceased in the mid-1940s. The bakehouse has long gone but the house still stands as 46 The Street. (Mildenhall Museum)

The Street, *c.* 1900. No. 10, on the right, was then used as a shop; later it became a house of ill repute! Church Meadow was built behind the wall on the left in the 1960s. (Mildenhall Museum)

A village wedding reception at Barton Hall, 1906. The bride is Lottie Turner and the groom is Walter Fish. The hall, now known as Middlefield Manor, is owned by the National Autistic Society as a home for young adults. (Miss F. Rutterford)

May Day was celebrated in great style with the local children donning fancy dress for the day as this 1909 group shows. Only a few names are known. In the front row, second from the left, is Augusta Rainbird; then come Jessie Rainbird and Lewis Grinwood. Fourth from the right is Edie Hockley and far right is Florence Gregory. (Mildenhall Museum)

All the names are known for the school group, above right. Back row, left to right: Miss Parker (later Mrs Spooner), Fitches, Smith, Dora Smith, Vicky and Bill Turner, Peter Amis, Percy, Ethel and Daisy Grimwood. Middle: Frances Smith, Lewis Nicholas, Arthur Smith, Florence Fitches, Kitty Witterton, Jack Crick, Nell Hicks, Butcher. Front: Bill Owers, William Peachey, Charles Edwards, Wilderston, Maud, Flossie and Ernest Smith, Mary, Jessie and Happy Rainbird, Muriel Rutterford.

The harvest group below right shows the following. Back row, left to right: George Owers, George Darkin, William Munns, George Race, Charlie Crick, Frank Turner. Middle: Jack Fitches, Ernie Cross, Mrs Hicks, Mrs Bentick, Fred Fitches, James Marshall, George Smith, Mrs Finch, Mr Turner, Mrs Turner, Mr Smith senior. Front: Mrs Fitches, Mrs Crick, Mrs Cornell, Mrs Rutterford, Turner, the boy standing.

A village school group, 1907. The National School in The Street was founded in 1845, but it is thought that there was once a second school in the village. (Mildenhall Museum)

All dressed up and ready for the music at an annual horkey, the local name for a harvest feast, 30 September 1910. The men all worked for Mr P. Burrell at Grange Farm. This may have been taken outside The Lamb. (Mildenhall Museum)

Peachey's Farm, also known as Thompson's Farm, on the Worlington to Tuddenham road, *c.* 1900. The buildings remained until 1968. (Mildenhall Museum)

Meadow View, on the main Tuddenham road, *c.* 1900. The names of the ladies are not known. It is believed that this was once a Methodist chapel but it may also have been a school. (Mildenhall Museum)

SECTION THREE
Beck Row

Beck Row has expanded greatly in order to provide housing for servicemen from RAF Mildenhall, but many traces of the old village remain and there is a very active community association. The Great Air Race from England to Australia started from here just before the base was officially opened in 1934 and King George V visited in 1935 for a full review of the Royal Air Force. The United States Air Force arrived in 1950 and the airfield is now expanding as other American installations in the United Kingdom are being run down. The local economy now depends heavily on the base, especially as so many British people are employed there and at nearby RAF Lakenheath.

The old Bird in Hand, with Ruth King at the door and Sam King standing with two unknown ladies, 1920s. The new hotel was built close by in the late 1930s. The old building continued as a private house for a while but was demolished in the 1940s. (Mr W. Bell)

A peaceful scene in The Street, 1908. It would be suicidal to stand in the middle of the road in this fashion today. Why were they doing so then? (Mildenhall Museum)

St John's House for Girls, opposite the church, probably 1920s. It was run by the Society for Providing Homes for Waifs and Strays and in 1884 housed twelve girls. This later became a private house but is now the Busy Bees Nursery School. (Mrs C. Crane)

Memorial Corner, 1930s. The war memorial stood at the corner of The Street and Holmsey Green but was moved along the road to its present site in about 1951. The names of the dead of the Second World War have yet to be added. (Mildenhall Museum)

The memorial for the men of Beck Row, Holywell Row and Wilde Street was dedicated on 3 July 1919. The salute was taken by Arthur Mothersole, the headmaster then of West Row School and later of the new Riverside School, who had won the military medal during the war. (Mr J. Haylock)

King George V's silver jubilee in 1935 was celebrated throughout the land, not least at Beck Row where 365 aircraft, representing thirty-eight squadrons of the Royal Air Force, were drawn up for review at the new RAF Mildenhall aerodrome. More local celebrations were organized by the committee which is seen here outside the village school, the windows of which have altered somewhat since this time. Back row, left to right: Arnold Clements, Algy Butcher, Walter Martin, Fred Clements, Mr Fenton, Don Haylock. Middle: John Peachey, ex-Sgt Hurrell, Don Clements, Mr P. Oldman, Chas Clements, Archie Morley, Jimmy Holland, Will Robbins. Front: Mrs John Peachey, Sam Parker, Mr Hawkins, Robert Fincham, Miss Thackery, Mrs Ed Fincham. (Mrs B. Bond)

The church Sunday school anniversary celebrations at Aspal Close, July 1908. The treat, typical of so many in the area, started with a procession of decorated horse-drawn wagons taking the children to a suitable spot for games and tea. (Mr L. Reeve)

Jack Rolfe of Aspal Lane, seen here at Barton Mills in the 1920s, used to follow all the Sunday school treats in the area, selling ice creams at ½d and 1d each to those who could afford such luxuries. He gave up the business in 1932 when work on the new RAF base became available. (Mildenhall Museum)

Aspal Hall farmhouse, at the bottom of Aspal Lane, *c.* 1900. Aspal Hall was one of the four ancient manors of Mildenhall. The house, for long the home of the Fincham family, was demolished in 1963, but traces of the old moat still remain. (Mildenhall Museum)

The Rose and Crown in Holmsey Green soon after the new pub was built in 1938. The group includes the landlady, Grace Spraggins. The old building still stands behind the modern part. (Mildenhall Museum)

SECTION FOUR

Cavenham

This small village, 4½ miles from Mildenhall, once had its own school, pub and post office but only the latter now remains. The prehistoric Icknield Way crosses the village and the Black Ditches, the remains of ancient boundaries, are listed as ancient monuments. The famous Cavenham crowns were found on the heath, which is now an important nature reserve. The Goldschmidt family, founders of Cavenham Foods, owned almost the entire village until 1918. The Suffolk Show was held here in 1954.

The village pub, The Plough, 1946. This, the only pub in the village, closed in about 1969 and is now a private house in a dry village. (Mr R. Gough)

Cavenham Hall, 1946. The house, built in 1898, had thirteen bedrooms and was set in grounds of 103 acres with a lake. It proved impossible to find a use for the property and it was demolished in 1949. (Mr R. Gough)

Park Farm, 1946. This was then a dairy farm of 597 acres. Mr J. Everett, the farm bailiff, lived here and part of the six bedroom house was used as the estate office. (Mr R. Gough)

SECTION FIVE

Eriswell

The village of Eriswell was owned in the eighteenth century by the Society for the Propagation of the Gospel in New England and many of the buildings still bear the letters NEC for New England Company. The society brought a Red Indian boy to the village and apprenticed him to a carpenter, but he died after only two years; his tombstone has recently been restored. The village later became incorporated in the great Elveden estate, owned from 1863 by the Maharajah Duleep Singh, the exiled Black Prince. The 1st Lord Iveagh, of the Guinness brewing family, bought the estate in the 1890s and it is still held by his heirs. The ruins of the church of St Peter are to be found at Eriswell Hall Farm.

Sparks Corner, 1920s. Mill Farm on the left and Sparks Farm on the right can still be seen, complete with their thatch, but this is now a busy junction on the main route between RAF Mildenhall and RAF Lakenheath. The little green with the old-fashioned signpost has long gone. (Mr W. Bell)

Until recent times almost all of the local men were employed on the estate. Here we see the villagers preparing to go to nearby Elveden for the annual horkey in 1898. Pearman Smith is driving the engine. Standing, left to right: W.J. Lock, the engine boy then aged seventeen, 'Daddy' Baker, the estate carpenter, Arthur Rudland, John Tripp, head cowman at Chamberlain's Farm, James Sale, first foreman at Chamberlain's Farm, Brown Rudland, the foreman carpenter. (Mildenhall Museum)

Taking a break from milking at Eriswell Hall, 1906 or 1907. Note the large pails. Left to right: Jack Nunn, -?-, Robert Hanslip, W. Palmer, -?-, Rodney Hanslip. The child is young Reg Hanslip, son of the Robert in the photograph. (Mr R. Hanslip)

Carting rye from Chalk Pit Field, at the top of Field Lane, early 1920s. Left to right: -?-, Robert Capp, -?-, David Cummings, Reg Hanslip and Charlie Turner with the horses. (Mr R. Hanslip)

The village cricket team, *c.* 1931. Standing, left to right: W. King (umpire), Reg Brunning, Walter Taylor, Eric Taylor, William Watton, Fred Worby, Charlie King (scorer). Seated: H.G.H. Wright, Jack Wortley, Harold Taylor, William Heffer, Reg Hanslip (vice-captain), William Lock (captain). (Mr R. Hanslip)

A cottage in Little London, probably 1920s. The lady is Jane Shinn and the man is presumably her husband. Why did both Eriswell and nearby Isleham have areas called Little London? (Mrs C. Crane)

SECTION SIX

Freckenham

Until recently Freckenham was administered as a *peculiar* of the Bishop of Rochester rather than by the local church officials. This caused many complications, not least over the proving of wills, and there were frequently disputes with the abbey of Bury St Edmunds. One such was settled by agreeing to position the village's gallows on the boundary with Herringswell so that the abbot's men could watch any executions! The village contains the remains of extensive earthworks, now listed as an ancient monument, but it is unlikely that there was ever a stone castle here.

St Andrew's Church from across the Lee Brook, 1920s. The remains of the old defensive earthworks surround the top of the hill. (Mildenhall Museum)

Church Lane, 1920s. The group of five cottages on the left was condemned in 1936 but lived in until 1949, being demolished in 1951 to make way for the present bungalow. The cottages on the right were replaced by a new house in 1953. (Mr R. Entwistle)

Pound Corner, 1920s. The present green in the road marks the site of the old pound where stray animals were kept. Pound Cottage, on the right, remains but the row of three cottages on the left has long since disappeared. (Mrs K. Gee)

The village street, 1920s. The second house on the right and the first on the left have long since been replaced by modern buildings. The village hall, built in 1894, has changed little over the years. (Mrs K. Gee)

Further along the street, showing the old bridge over the river, 1920s. The old forge on the left has been replaced by The Street garage. (Mrs K. Gee)

The mill on the Fordham road, 1905. The remains of a second mill can still be seen off the Chippenham road. (Mrs K. Gee)

Mortimer's Lane, named after a medieval landowner, 1920s. The old cottage has been preserved although it has lost its thatched roof. (Mildenhall Museum)

SECTION SEVEN

Herringswell

The tiny one-street village of Herringswell is somewhat off the beaten track and receives few chance visitors, although it is well worth exploring the interesting church of St Ethelbert, rapidly restored after the fire of 25 February 1869. One occasional visitor in the past was the Earl of Arundel who once owned the manor; there was an unusual custom that he should be offered a joint of bacon, held on the tip of a lance, whenever he passed through the village. A less welcome arrival was that of the Medina Rajneesh sect, which occupied Herringswell Manor from 1982 when the American boarding school there closed. The colourful orange and yellow robes of the members brightened the country lanes but local folk were shocked by the rumours of free love within the community and were relieved when the sect departed, being replaced in 1986 by the Shi-Tennoji Buddhist School; the Japanese boarders add a touch of the exotic without causing offence.

An early view of the post office in The Street. This was probably taken before or during the First World War as there is a large recruiting poster for the guards to the right of the door. (Mildenhall Museum)

The Beehive in The Street, probably before the First World War. This unusual cottage still stands although it has lost its thatch and has been extended. (Mildenhall Museum)

The procession for the village carnival, 3 August 1908. Herringswell, despite its small population, continues to hold regular events of this nature. (Mr L. Reeve)

Holywell Row

An unusual feature of Holywell Row is that the Quakers, or Society of Friends, had a meeting house here from about as early as 1678, only some two years after James Webb of Mildenhall was fined for having a meeting in his house. The early Friends were poor and could only afford a barn-like structure some 50 ft long and 25 ft wide. However, they were evidently more prosperous by 1759 when they built a 6 ft high brick wall around the graveyard, the earliest headstone in which is dated 1698, by which time the meeting house had been tiled and extended. They were doubtless hampered in their early years by Francis Bugg of Mildenhall, a local shopkeeper who renounced Quakerism and wrote a total of sixteen books attacking the movement. The local Methodists were allowed to lease the chapel in 1875 and now own the property.

The ruins of the old Quaker meeting house alongside the modern Methodist chapel, 1967. The new chapel was built in 1955 and the old one was demolished in the 1970s. (Mildenhall Museum)

Holywell Row may be small but it could once boast its own silver band. This was active before the First World War but petered out between the wars. The instruments were hung up in the village hall for many years but they gradually disappeared one by one. Back row, left to right: Tom Stebbeds, Bill Morley, Henry Curtis, Fred Stebbeds, Freddie Dewers. Front: Herbert Stebbeds, Frank Pole, the bandmaster William Haylock, Fritz Golding, Tom Stirges. Fred Stebbeds' son Frank relates how Fred was once playing his euphonium so enthusiastically that he blew out the gas light above him. (Mildenhall Museum)

The village had its own post office, seen here in the 1920s, until 1949. The old building, run for many years by the Haylock family, is now a private house, 34 The Street. (Mildenhall Museum)

The bungalows, 52–6 The Street, 1936. They were built in the 1920s and occupied by, from the left, Archie Morley, Frank Powell, William Morley and Mr Peachey. The man with the cart is Charlie Woollard. (Mildenhall Museum)

The West End (of Holywell Row, not London), 1936. The cottage on the left was demolished in 1974 to enlarge the entrance to Laurel Farm. The ladies, from the left, are Alice Farthing, Mrs Dick Webb and Mrs Florrie Wiseman. (Mildenhall Museum)

Joseph and Rose Clements outside their cottage, 1920s. This had been derelict for many years when it was demolished in 1964. Laurel Farm bungalow, 12 The Street, now stands here. (Mrs C. Crane)

SECTION NINE

Icklingham

The remains of an extensive Roman settlement, including the earliest known building set aside for Christian worship, have been excavated in Icklingham, and at nearby West Stow an Anglo-Saxon village has been reconstructed. The wealth and importance of the area in former times is confirmed by there being two parishes in the village, each with its own church – at either end of the main street and not, as at Swaffham Prior, set in one churchyard. The church of St James was completely restored in 1864 and remains in use; that of All Saints escaped the attention of the well-meaning Victorians and retains many original features, including a thatched roof, but is now redundant and opened only for occasional services.

An early view of Marston's original mill from across the river. Only Icklingham, of all the villages covered in this book, still has a working mill. (Mrs P. Gower)

The Red Lion, 1904. Mr R.T. Allfrey was then the landlord, having succeeded Charles Wing who, in the 1890s, had hoped to build a wharf at the rear of the property when the Lark was being reopened for navigation. (Mr J. Gates)

The Hall, taken from across the street, 1960s. WAAFS, and later prisoners of war, were accommodated here during the Second World War. After the war it was divided into nine flats before being demolished in 1969. (Mrs P. Gower)

Looking west along The Street, probably before the First World War. The vast bulk of The Hall, now the site of The Hall Close, can be seen on the right. (Mildenhall Museum)

The Plough, when George Fitches was the landlord, 1906. There were three other pubs in the village at this time: The Bell, The Crown and The Red Lion. (Mildenhall Museum)

Ivy Cottage in The Street, 1916 or 1917. By the cart is Joe Palmer with Bill Partridge on the cart. The soldier in the doorway is Archie Rainbird. The girls are Ivy Naylor (later Mrs Linney) and Cissy Sladden (Mrs Taylor). (Mrs P. Gower)

An early view of The Street showing the dispensary on the left. This, endowed by Alice Dix, finally closed in June 1993, having in its latter years functioned as a branch surgery for the Mildenhall practice. (Mrs P. Gower)

The post office and shop, 1905. Unfortunately, like so many villages nowadays, Icklingham is bereft of these facilities. (Mildenhall Museum)

The Bury bus outside the post office, c. 1920. The postmaster, Mr Naylor, is standing outside the post office and his wife is in the bus, the face on the extreme left. This bus, as the board shows, ran from Mildenhall to Bury through all the villages. (Mildenhall Museum)

The junction of The Street and West Street, *c.* 1900. The house on the right remains but that on the left has long since gone, so widening the lane to the mill. The end of the churchyard wall and the front of the school, closed in 1988, can be seen. (Mrs P. Gower)

The thatched cottages have been removed to be replaced by 19–21 West Street but the house beyond the cottages, formerly The Bell, still stands. This had been a pub for generations but finally closed because of lack of custom in 1969. (Mrs P. Gower)

Kenny Hill

There is no true hill at Kenny Hill, which is set well into the fenland part of the old Mildenhall parish. The fens used to be a watery wilderness but some small islands remained dry for most of the year, and Kenny Hill was one of these. The land, which is now well drained and some of the most fertile in the country, used to support a sizeable farming community, but the advent of mechanization brought depopulation. The village at the turn of the century could boast its own church, school, football team and two pubs, The Labourer's Rest and The Rising Sun, but all of these have now been lost.

The Kenny Hill Wanderers football team outside The Labourer's Rest, 1920. Standing, left to right: Walter Martin, Jim Powell, Bert Cobbin, Jim Butcher, Russell Powell, Ted Fincham. Seated: Jack Webb, George Smith, Mr Smith Flanders, Perce Baker, Sam Large. Ernie Cobham is at the front. (Mildenhall Museum)

Charles Eagle Phillips in the garden of The Rising Sun, *c.* 1900. The large object, being used here to house beehives, is the steeple from the iron church at Kenny Hill which was blown down in a gale in 1895. No photographs of the church as a whole survive but at least we can see the steeple. Mr Phillips lived his entire life at The Rising Sun where he died, aged eighty-five, in 1920. (This photograph has always been catalogued as above but it has recently been suggested that the subject might be John Ford; it certainly shows the church steeple.) (Mildenhall Museum)

The train crash at Shippea Hill, 7 April 1906. The engine of the Norwich to Cambridge express, together with several carriages, left the rails but fortunately there were no serious injuries or fatalities. (Mildenhall Museum)

Cultivating on Henry Payne's farm, 1925. The horses are Blossom, Brisk and Depper but the name of the boy is not known. (Mildenhall Museum)

The Kenny Hill Coronation Committee, 26 June 1902. The crowning of Edward VII signalled the end of the Victorian era but the formal clothing seen here still has a nineteenth-century appearance. Standing, left to right: Riley Brand, Samuel Clark (churchwarden), John Sefton, -?-, Charles Fincham (head and shoulders only), Smith Flanders, Jake Butcher (head and shoulders), Walter Robb, Charles Phillips, John Phillips, Isaac Lenard, Mrs Ashman. Seated: George, Ben and Tom Ashman, Mr F.J. Payne (whose baby Henry can be seen behind Smith Flanders), Robert Sefton. (Mildenhall Museum)

SECTION ELEVEN

Tuddenham

The ancient Icknield Way runs through Tuddenham St Mary (so called to distinguish it from Tuddenham St Martin which is near Ipswich) and crosses the large nature reserve that was once held by the village on behalf of the poor. An airfield was constructed on the outskirts of the village in 1943 and was home to 90 Squadron RAF, equipped first with Stirlings and then with Lancasters, until 1946; a memorial to the squadron was placed on The Green in 1982. RAF Tuddenham closed for flying in November 1946 but was retained for possible later use and, from 1959, became a Thor missile site. All activity on the base ceased in 1963 and only ruins now remain. The services, however, left a permanent mark on the village for the High Street was metalled to accommodate the wartime traffic; previously it had been only a dirt road.

Mike Rudderham and his grandchildren, John, Susan and Jennifer Grimwood, stroll down The Green in the 1940s. A Lancaster can be seen coming in to land at the airfield. The old Reading Room on the left became defunct when the new village hall was built in 1955. (Mildenhall Museum)

The school on The Green, 1930s. The village has had a school since 1723. This building was erected in 1844 and became a national school in 1871. It was sold as a private house when the new school was built in 1962. (Mildenhall Museum)

Tuddenham Mill, 1953. This was built in 1775 and extended in 1863. Milling stopped in 1954 and the building has been used as a restaurant since 1973. Diners can watch the old wheel turning as they eat. (Mildenhall Museum)

This view shows Spooner's butcher's and general stores, *c.* 1900. Four generations of the family ran the business here from the 1860s to the 1970s when Mr W. Spooner moved to a shop opposite. The cottage at the far left was badly damaged by a bomb on 24 September 1940 and had to be taken down. (Mildenhall Museum)

This slightly later view looks the other way down the High Street. The cottage in the middle left has disappeared but all the other buildings remain. The post office was then in one of the houses on the right, not in the shop in the foreground. (Mildenhall Museum)

A seed drill was said to have been blown on to the roof of a shed at Hill Farm in the blizzard of 28 March 1916. Was this a genuine event or an elaborate practical joke? (Mildenhall Museum)

Daniel Williams of Higham Road, *c*. 1930. He was one of the last shepherds in the area to wear the old-fashioned, but very practical, smock. (Mildenhall Museum)

West Row

West Row was until recently part of the parish of Mildenhall but, in terms of population and prosperity, has often been a rival to the High Town itself. William Coe, who died in 1729, was a wealthy farmer who often visited the Cock Inn in Mildenhall to drink and play cards late at night with Sir Thomas Hanmer and other local gentry. His diary, which is being published by the Suffolk Records Society, records the many accidents that nearly happened to him and his determination to give up his sinful habits. Simpson records that on 14 February 1700 Mr Eldred, a barber from Bury, cut off the hair of Coe's three daughters, Judith, Anne and Elizabeth; then, on 7 May, the hair was returned in the form of a wig for their father.

Mains water did not come to West Row until the 1940s. Trips to the well could be a social occasion if you did not have your own in the back garden. Here, in the 1920s, Evelyn Thompson (later Mrs Gort) on the left meets Mrs Sydney Rivett and Mrs Hannah 'Moody' Bassett at a well near the school. (Mr W. Bell)

The first batch of men, all volunteers, left West Row to serve in the First World War on 14 September 1914. Here they are, lined up between the pond and Beeches Farm. Their families were upset to see them go, not just because of the dangers they faced but also because many worked unpaid on the family farms. (Mildenhall Museum)

After the parade the volunteers were driven off to barracks. For many this must have been their first ride in a motor car. The cottage on the right is seen again in the photographs opposite. (Mildenhall Museum)

The village pond, 1950s. The houses on the left survive but the pond dried out in the 1960s. Many still remember the joys of skating here. (Mildenhall Museum)

Frank and Hetty Hinds with their son Godfrey outside their shop, 13 Beeches Road, 1930s. Frank's brother Arthur had taken over their father's shop in Friday Street and Frank had branched out on his own. (Mildenhall Museum)

Beeches Road, with Morley's garage on the right, 1940s. The middle house on the left has been replaced by a bungalow but the others remain. (Mildenhall Museum)

Flooding outside Morley's garage, *c.* 1930. The girl in the centre is Elsie Norman (later Mrs Taylor-Balls) holding her baby sister Una. The middle house, also seen above, has been lost. (Mildenhall Museum)

Richard Rolfe and his daughter May (later Mrs Frank Ford) outside the village post office and wheelwright's yard, *c.* 1915. This site later became Morley's bus garage and is now Taylor-Balls' yard. The saw yard is seen below. (Mildenhall Museum)

The saw yard, 1921. Left to right: Richard Rolfe, Frank Phillips, Arthur Rivett, Victor Rumbelow, Jack Thompson. Harry Butcher is the driver of the famous 'Woofer' engine, probably then the oldest Burrell general purpose engine still working. (Mr A.J. Thompson)

The forge at 19 Beeches Road, 1904. Left to right: Newman Ford, Arthur Ford, Mrs Sally Ford, Dick Webb, Billy Ford, Jesse Ford the blacksmith and, holding the horses, George Mackender. Iron tyres for cartwheels are being heated on a turf fire. (Mildenhall Museum)

Another view of the forge, 1906. The old post office can be seen on the far side of the road. Left to right: Billy Ford, Elsie Ford (later Mrs Phillips), Mrs Sally Ford, Doris Evelyn Ford (later Mrs Rolfe), Dick Webb, George Mackender, Newman Ford. (Mildenhall Museum)

W.J. Ford's engineering works, *c.* 1906. Left to right: -?-, Ted Ford, Cornelius Brown, Clark Brown, Sydney Ford, George Butcher, Noakes Ford and William Ford whose children are at the front. The Burrell Boydell engine of about 1857 is in for repair. The famous Mildenhall Treasure, a hoard of Roman silver now in the British Museum, was ploughed up at nearby Gage Farm during the Second World War by Gordon Butcher who was working for Syd Ford. Butcher and Ford took the thirty-two pieces back to the workshop where Ford straightened out the buckled dishes so well that the British Museum experts had little to do when they received the collection after a treasure trove inquest was held in 1946. (Mr A.J. Thompson)

The junction with The Green, *c.* 1910. The Methodist chapel on the corner was opened in 1841 but closed in 1956 and is now Berrycroft Stores; the gravestones remain in front of the shop. The buildings of Bedlam Yard can be seen on the right. (Mildenhall Museum)

Bedlam Yard, properly known as Chapel Yard, 1915. Before the First World War as many as fifty people lived here in some eight cottages. Some of the buildings remain but in a derelict state. David Abrey, who died in 1991, was the last man to live here. (Mr W. Bell)

Next down The Green came The Elms, since demolished to make way for Mr T. Water's large modern bungalow. This family group of about 1910 shows, from the left, Annie Jarman, Bessie Norman, Mrs Annie Jarman and Arthur Jarman. (Mr W. Bell)

Arthur Hinds' grocery and drapery shop at 101 Friday Street, *c.* 1934. At the front is Diana Taylor Balls (later Mrs Finnegan); then, from the left, Mary Fendick, Arthur Hinds, Aldwyth Morley (Mrs Palmer), Mrs Georgina Hinds and Mr Hills. (Mildenhall Museum)

The village fire brigade, outside the Barley Barn (which has since been converted to the cottages at 10–14 Beeches Road), 1890s. Left to right: Noakes Ford, Harry Hayes, Jesse Ford, George Gittus, William Ford, Fred Balls, another William Ford, Walter Boyce, Abraham Ford, John Ford, Fred Gittus, Arthur Rivett. The boys are Ted and Adolphus Ford. (Mildenhall Museum)

Mr Butler's fish shop in Beeches Road, 1920s. This, and the adjacent fire engine house, were burned down in about 1930. Left to right: Cyril Webb, Mr A. Butler, Gordon Webb, Clarke Morley. Note the fire hook on the wall. (Mr W. Bell)

The West Row band, 27 August 1949. Back row, left to right: Ivan Morley, Cyril Isaacson, Keith Butler, Len Aves, M. Bridge, C. Eaglen. Middle: D. Isaacson, Raymond Butcher, A. Payne, Frank Aves, T. Quinn, R. Isaacson, Frank Ford, Doug Ingle. Front: Gerald King, Trevor Bell, Mr Hermen, Bert Hearn, Ivor Rolfe, Bert Isaacson, Clifford Forman. The band was first formed in November 1948 with Bert Isaacson as bandmaster, Gerald King as treasurer and Bert Hearn as secretary. (Mr W. Bell)

One of the classes at West Row School, 28 April 1914. Back row, left to right: Bessie Clarke (later Mrs Norman), Ernie Jarman, Charlie Norman, Alban Taylor, Frank Webb, Albert Keeble, Victor Smith, Albert Mendham, George Bassett, Luther Morley, Walter Morley. Middle: Maud Halls, Ada Morley, Annie Bassett, Lily Harding, Millie Mackender, Dolly Morris, Violet Morris, -?-, Leonard Aves, Gordon Frost. Front: Jessie Halls, Freda Morley, Marjorie Abrey, Sarah Bassett, Florence Chapman, Edie Mason, Eppie Mason, Tilly Nicholas, Jessie Nicholas. This school opened in 1874. St Peter's Church was then created by adding a chancel to the old school building. (Mr W. Bell)

Outside the headmaster's house, 26 May 1908. By the door are Freda Norman and the headmaster, Mr Hayes. Left to right: Nellie Fowler, Bessie Norman, Freda Hayes, Mrs Hayes, Daphne Hayes, Julie Clarke (later Mrs Woollard), Annie Jarman (Mrs Bell), Nellie Rolfe (Mrs Ingle). (Mr W. Bell)

The Mildenhall Fen Council School stood on the river bank at the top of Engine Drove. This 1908 scene shows a surprisingly attractive classroom. The teacher at the back is Emma Clark (later Mrs Newman Ford), and Miss Fanny Flack is by the window. (Mildenhall Museum)

The West Row Baptists practised open-air total immersion and made use of the river at Judes Ferry. Here, on 19 July 1914, the Revd C.J. Fowler is assisted by Charles Abrey; the subject is probably Nellie Jaggard. The last baptism here was celebrated in 1932. (Mr W. Bell)

A butter-making competition outside The White Horse, c. 1912. Butter-making classes and competitions were quite regular events. The gentleman is the Revd C.J. Fowler, the Baptist minister. The lady on the far left is Mrs Lock. (Mildenhall Museum)

The annual Baptist Sunday school treats were great events. A procession of decorated carts and cyclists made its way through Beck Row and Mildenhall, often to Street Farm at Barton Mills where this view was taken in 1908. (Mr W. Bell)

The Church of England and Wesleyan Sunday schools had their own separate outings. This postcard, one of a series published in 1908, shows that the local carrier, J.R. Baker, had lent his wagon for the day. His horses look as though they could have done with the day off. (Mildenhall Museum)

The tent pegging demonstration team at the West Row flower show and sports, 20 July 1911. This annual show rivalled that of Mildenhall itself. (Mr L. Reeve)

The tug of war at the sports day, 20 July 1911. The man with the watch chain is Bob Peachey, a builder from Barton Mills. The carousel is Crighton's pony roundabout, flying horses driven by a pony. (Mildenhall Museum)

Few could afford the luxury of a car in the early days. This Model T Ford, seen with Bargate Farm in the background, is being driven by James Dunlop of Beeches Farm. Dick Rolfe, the undertaker, is in the middle and William J. Ford, the engineer, is on the right. (Mr W. Bell)

The Bell family from Weston Ditch, 1920s. Most people had to rely on their feet and were lucky if they could afford a horse and cart. Left to right: George Bell, George Cooper (with apologies to Alf Garnett), Philip Bell, David Bell. (Mildenhall Museum)

These picturesque, at least on the outside, cottages stood at the junction of Cricks Road and Church Road until the 1940s. Mrs Harry Morley and Miss Hannah Coe can just be seen at the gate in this view of about 1910. (Mr W. Bell)

Eldo Road, before the First World War. The cottage in the middle was knocked down to make way for a new house for Mr Sheldrick and later all were demolished to make way for Taylor-Balls' transport yard. Juniper Gardens now occupy the site. (Mr W. Bell)

The Morley family outside their farmhouse, *c.* 1895. Left to right: Samuel Morley, Mrs Morley, Shed Morley, George Morley and their maid, Esther Baker or Bacon from Beck Row. The house later burnt down and Church Gardens were built here. (Mildenhall Museum)

This photograph of Grandfather Samuel Morley may, judging by his youthful appearance compared with that above, be as old as the 1850s. He was a seedsman and used to make a trip to Bury Market every Wednesday. (Mildenhall Museum)

Potato picking at Mons Plantation, just before the First World War. Left to right: Charles Jarman, George Bell, Sam Bassett, Simon Ingle, Jim Stone, George Coe, Arthur Ellington, Arthur Norman. The hedge in the background marks the line of the Old Way, a wide cattle drove that crossed the land now occupied by the airfield. (Mildenhall Museum)

Worlington

The small village of Worlington is renowned for its golf course, said to be the finest nine hole course in the country. The club was founded in 1893 and granted its present title, the Royal Worlington and Newmarket Golf Club, by Queen Victoria in 1895. The village was formerly divided into two manors which were obviously in competition in the thirteenth century when both obtained royal permission to hold weekly markets and annual fairs. These, if ever they were actually held, have long since gone.

The village war memorial, 1921. Church Lane leads off to the left and Bell Lane to the right. Until the council houses were built in Church Lane in the 1930s there was a clear view from here to the church. Virginia Cottage can be seen on the left. (Mrs M. Powell)

Outside The Bell, 1915. Left to right: -?-, -?-, -?-, Charles, Gordon and Mrs Phillips, -?-, Agnes and Tom Hood with their children, -?-, -?-, Polly Phillips, young Phyllis Phillips (later Mrs Morley), Annie Laurie Jeffrey. The Bell closed in 1967. (Mrs P. Morley)

A traction engine belonging to Parker Brothers of Mildenhall outside The Bell, c. 1920. On the left is the driver, George Smith, and on the right is Bill Gage. This Garrett no. 4 compound engine was bought in January 1916 for £550. (Mildenhall Museum)

Ecclestone's of Mildenhall making a delivery of groceries in Church Lane, *c.* 1920. The van is a Model T Ford with Harold Hunt as driver and young Phillips of Barton Mills as mate. The cottages are little changed: on the left is Poulter's Farm and on the right Tudor Cottage and Baker's Cottage. (Mr W. Bell)

Walnut Cottage, seen here in the early 1900s, was set back next to Poulter's Farm in Church Lane by the entrance to the Nut Meadow on which Walnut Grove was built in 1967. This cottage, for long the home of the Thornalley family, was pulled down in 1969. (Mrs M. Powell)

Rose Cottage and the old post office before the First World War. The lady at the door is probably Mrs Charlotte Palmer. A modern house now stands here. The post office later moved opposite to The Kernels in the old building that can still be seen. It moved to its present site in 1933 and the new shop was built in 1965. (Mildenhall Museum)

This view of The Street, also taken before the First World War, shows Rose Cottage and the old post office in the middle right. Tye Beam Cottage, to the left of the post office, still stands. The Grove, on the right, has hardly changed over the years. (Mildenhall Museum)

The village school group photograph, 1926. The school was opened in 1840 and could cater for sixty children but by the 1890s the average attendance was only thirty-eight and there are only twenty-eight in this group. It closed in 1959 and is now a private house. This view was taken in the school yard; Lark Close was built behind the fence in 1967–8. Front row, left to right: John Collen, Jim Rose, Douglas Pooley, Victor Phillips, Charles Smith, Desmond Jarvis, Frank Pooley, Ron Hibble. Second row: Kath Roberts (later Mrs Gowers), Grace Pooley (Mrs Snell), Barbara Sizer (Mrs Jaggard), Mary Williams, Freda Phillips, Betty Butcher (Mrs Grant), Vera Shinn, Joyce Aldous, Jean Sizer, Jean Thornalley (Mrs Lucas). Standing: Douglas Butcher, Molly Thornalley (Mrs Powell), Reg Sizer, Doris Thornalley (Mrs Butcher), possibly a Gould, Rosie Shinn (Mrs Richardson), Phyllis Shinn (Mrs Carter), possibly a Coe, Bruce Laws, Richard Phillips. Back row: Miss Florrie Hinard, the headmistress, Leslie Baker, Miss MacCardoff. (Mrs M. Powell)

The Chequers, with Mr Holland's milk cart from Rectory Farm making a delivery, early 1920s. The cottages just beyond the pub were taken down in 1967; 'Old Barratt' kept a shop in the first cottage until the late 1920s. Manor Farm can be seen further along on the left. (Mildenhall Museum)

Edward Howell kept the blacksmith's shop on the corner opposite The Chequers. He must be one of the figures in this photograph, which dates from about 1900. The cottage is still standing. (Mrs P. Morley)

The Worlington section of the Mildenhall Company of the Home Guard, taken outside Zealandia House, *c.* 1945. Standing, left to right: George Henry Baker, Leslie Baker, George Wisbey, Jack Leverington, Sid Sykes, George Rutter, Alec Foster. Seated: John Collen, Albert Collen, Harold Sizer, George Thornalley senior, Arthur Nicholas, Jack Devonshire, Frank Pooley. There had been a very real fear that invasion would strike across East Anglia. Lines of concrete pill-boxes were hastily erected and many can still be seen today, as can the base for a spigot mortar in the old Mildenhall cemetery. (Mrs M. Powell)

Acknowledgements

Firstly I must express my gratitude to the trustees of the Mildenhall Museum for allowing me use of their extensive collection of local material. Then, on behalf of the trustees, I must thank the many people who have given photographs to the museum over the years. I have not acknowledged these donors individually as copies have often arrived from more than one source. Otherwise the owner of each photograph is acknowledged in the captions. I have been privileged to have been allowed access to many private collections, some almost as large as the museum's holdings, and trusted to borrow material for months on end. It would have been impossible to have finished this book without the help of these collectors and also of those many people who have so willingly provided me with information. Sometimes there have been differing views on the details of certain photographs and I have had to weigh up the evidence; I must take final responsibility for the facts and opinions that I have given but I will always remain open to correction. The generosity shown by Miss Cissie Simpson in bequeathing her family's volumes of Simpson's Mildenhall Directories and Monthly Magazines to the Mildenhall Museum has made checking of details so much easier and reference is made to these works in several captions. Finally, I must express my heartfelt thanks to my wife who has put up with our dining-room table being permanently covered by photographs and books without complaint and who, in the later stages of editing, has acted as my detective and messenger on many occasions. This book could not have been completed without her patience and support.